# The Beautiful Book of

# QUESTIONS

Laine Cunningham

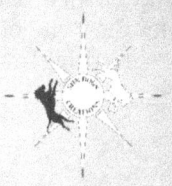

The Beautiful Book of Questions

Published by Sun Dogs Creations
*Changing the World One Book at a Time*

Print ISBN: 9781946732699

Cover Design by Angel Leya

Copyright © 2018 and 2019 Laine Cunningham

All rights reserved. No part of this book may be reproduced in any form or by any means, electronic, mechanical, digital, photocopying or recording, except for the inclusion in a review, without permission in writing from the publisher.

The

# BEAUTIFUL

# BOOK

# SERIES

Align Your Passion With Your Purpose

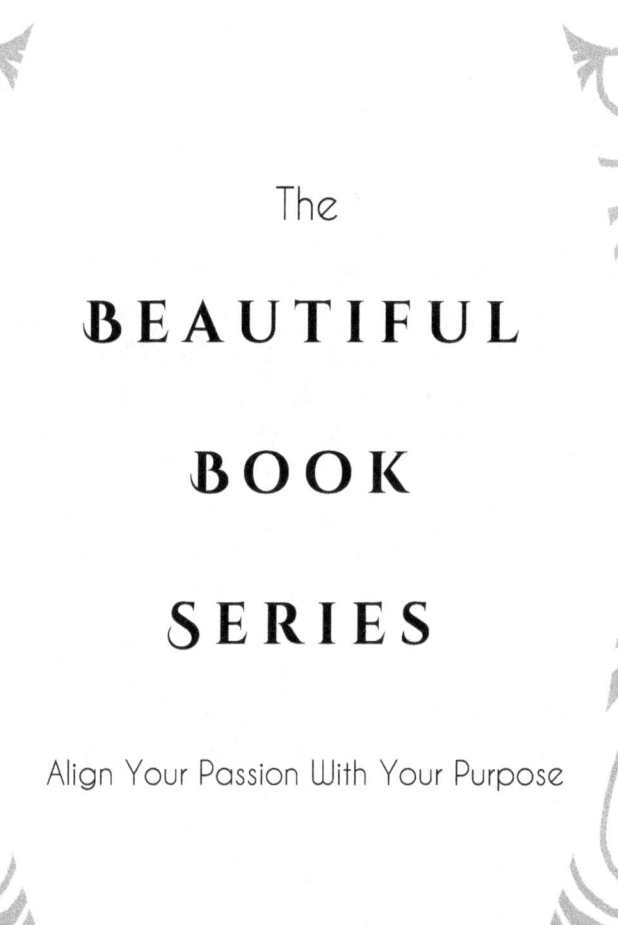

**WELCOME** to the first step in your new life!

No matter how old you are, no matter how much success you've already achieved, and no matter how many challenging issues you face, you can change everything. You can harness the best of what you know and chart a new course. The skills you have mastered and your natural abilities can create the beautiful life of your dreams.

*The Beautiful Book of Questions* is the beacon that will shine a brilliant, illuminating light on your life. On these pages, you will explore three crucial reference points: your past, your present, and your beautiful future.

Questions about your past explore who you have been and what you have achieved. You will recognize all the skills you can call on to build your brightest future.

Prompts about your present reveal where you are now in terms of your life goals. You will also be reminded of the strengths that brought you to this place.

The questions that turn you toward your future show you the richness and love that can be yours. The areas where you can get more out of your life will blaze like stars.

Page through this book whenever you reach a milestone like a career change or other big event. When you find yourself wondering how to handle an issue, answer the questions again. Record your answers to keep your beautiful future in focus at all times.

The simple and effective questions in *The Beautiful Book of Questions* will probe just the right spot at just the right time. If nothing arises right away, simply move on. Your subconscious will surprise you by providing the answer when you need it most!

*Are you lost or are you exploring?*

*Who are you becoming?*

*Can your definition of success be adjusted?*

*What advice would you offer your newborn self?*

*If you could control your
nightly dreams,
what impossible thing
would you do?*

*Is the obstacle
actually an opportunity?*

*When will you be satisfied with your achievements?*

*Do you sow so that others can reap?*

*What great kindness can you perform today?*

*Are you driven by need or by choice?*

*At which points will you pivot?*

*How will you define your best self?*

*What are you willing to forgo for now?*

*Which answers
do you seek?*

*Where will you seek?*

*What do you treasure above all else?*

*Who will walk beside you?*

*From whom should you step away?*

*What motivates you despite the odds?*

*Which outcome do you choose?*

*Which thoughts, ideas and beliefs should you carry?*

*What will you
plant along the way?*

*What will you trade in order to gain?*

*How will your perspective change?*

*What conflict must you resolve?*

*Which conflicts can you avoid?*

*What does transition look like to you?*

*At which speed should you travel?*

*Whom do you want to become?*

*What do you need right now?*

*How will you supply your own needs?*

*What will you sow?*

*What will you reap?*

*If you build it,
who will use it?*

*As you advance, when will you rest?*

*When will you begin?*

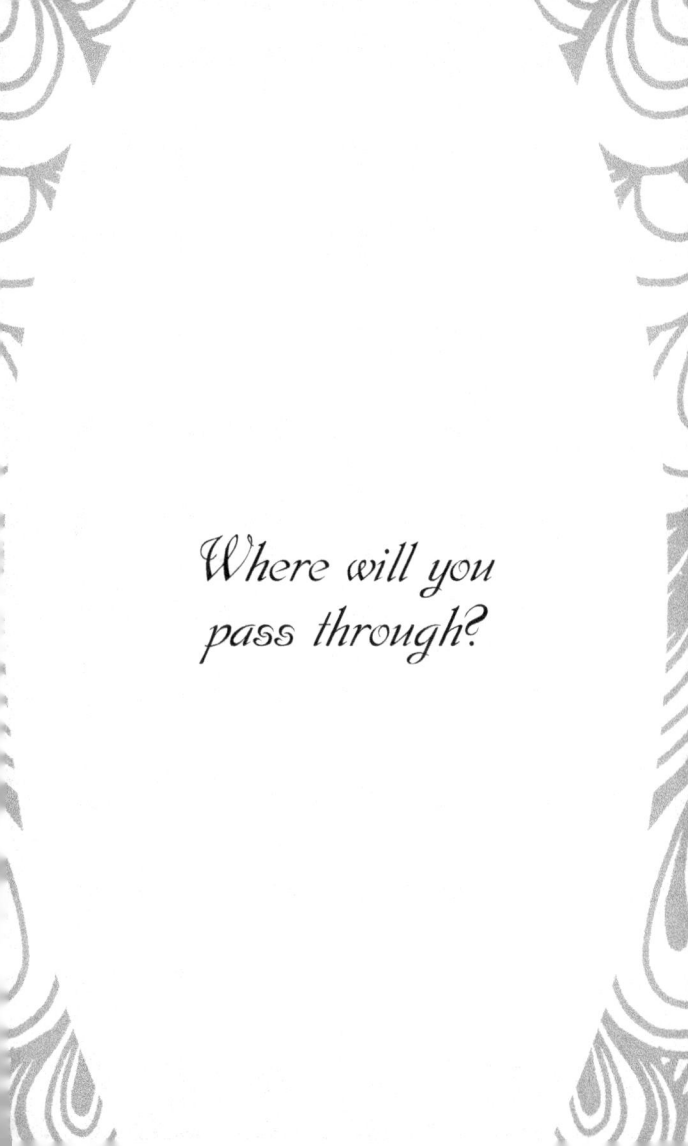

*Where will you pass through?*

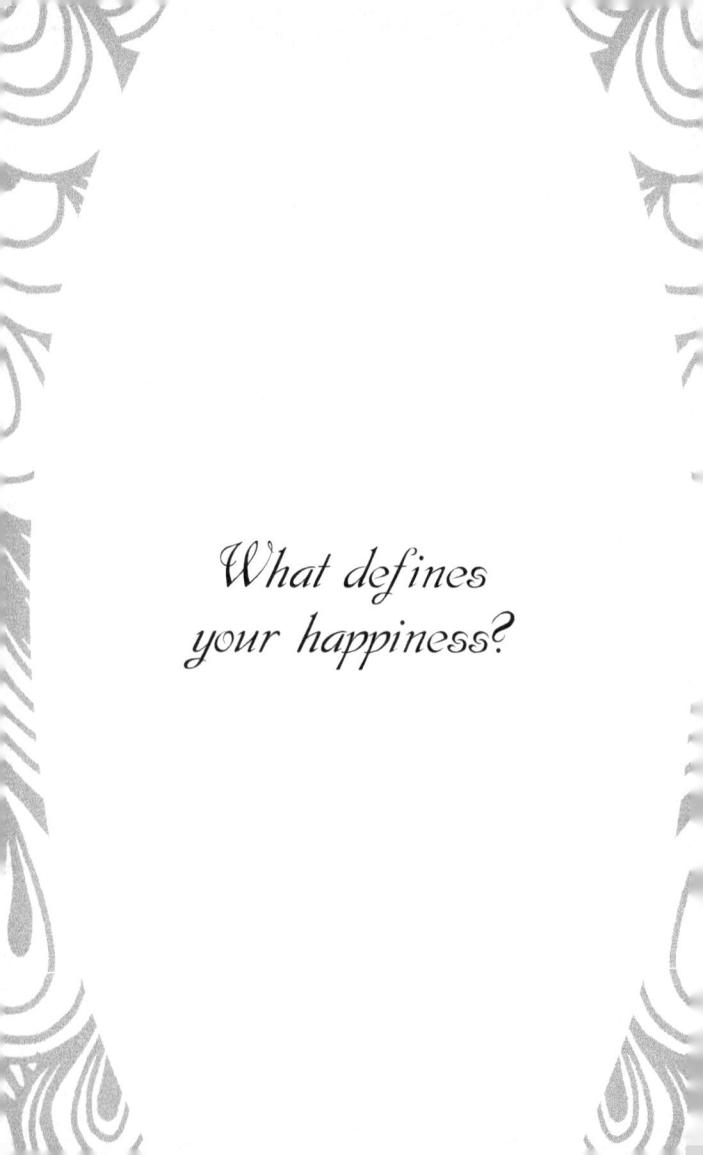

*What makes you proud?*

*What brings you joy?*

*How do you give joy to others?*

*Where will you find peace?*

*What obligations are not truly yours?*

*How sturdy is your foundation?*

*How do you define beauty?*

*What beauty do you recognize in yourself?*

*What beauty will you cultivate in the world?*

*How will success make you feel?*

*What whispers arise from your heart?*

*Which failures should you forgive?*

*When will you embrace your desires?*

*What have you already begun?*

*How will you celebrate each milestone?*

*What will be
the final reward?*

*How will
you change?*

*Who will
you help?*

*Which shortcuts are worth the risk?*

*When will you live fully?*

## NOVELS BY LAINE CUNNINGHAM

*The Family Made of Dust*

*Beloved*

*Reparation*

## OTHER BOOKS BY LAINE CUNNINGHAM

*Woman Alone: A Six-Month Journey Through the Australian Outback*

*On the Wallaby Track*

*Seven Sisters: Spiritual Messages from Aboriginal Australia*

*Writing While Female or Black or Gay*

*The Zen of Travel*
*The Zen of Gardening*
*Zen in the Stable*
*The Zen of Chocolate*
*The Zen of Dogs*

*The Wisdom of Puppies*
*The Wisdom of Babies*
*The Wisdom of Weddings*

*Bikes of Berlin*
*Necropolises of New Orleans I & II*
*Ruins of Rome I & II*
*Ancients of Assisi I & II*
*Panoramas of Portugal*
*Nuances of New York*
*Glimpses of Germany*
*Impressions of Italy*
*Altitudes of the Alps*
*Knights Through the Ages*
*Coast of California*
*Utopia of the Unicorn*
*Flourishes of France*
*Portraits of Paris*
*Tableaus of Tbilisi*
*Grandeur in the Republic of Georgia*

*The Beautiful Book of Questions*
*The Beautiful Book for Dream Seekers*
*The Beautiful Book for Rebels*
*The Beautiful Book for Women*
*The Beautiful Book for Lovers*

www.ingramcontent.com/pod-product-compliance
Lightning Source LLC
Chambersburg PA
CBHW071755080526
44588CB00013B/2238